MIRCEA CANTOR
THE NEED FOR UNCERTAINTY

MODERN ART OXFORD ARNOLFINI, BRISTOL CAMDEN ARTS CENTRE, LONDON

III ┃3 artists ┃3 spaces ┃3 years

CONTENTS

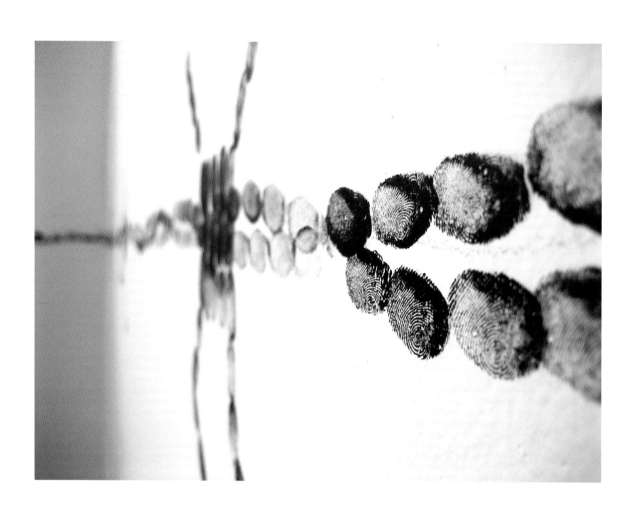

This and previous page:
Chaplet
2007
Printing ink, artist's fingerprints

FOREWORD

This publication has been created to accompany Mircea Cantor's *The Need for Uncertainty*, the first in a new series of three artists' commissions. Presented as a programme over three years, the 3 series is being produced as a partnership between Modern Art Oxford, Arnolfini, Bristol and Camden Arts Centre, London. All three institutions share a history and a commitment to presenting the work of contemporary artists at key moments in their career.

Our desire for the series is to enable three pioneering international artists to create a substantial new work and to make this work visible to audiences in the UK. Each of the commissioned works will be presented in Oxford, Bristol and London. At the end of their presentations, the commissioned works will be made available for acquisition by a regional public collection, contributing to the development of those collections and ensuring a legacy for the artists' work in this country.

The process of commissioning is central to the series. The opportunity to create new work in different contexts, and the expanded possibilities that this entails, has proved to be a vital stimulus for Mircea Cantor. The commissioning process also fosters a particular relationship between commissioner and artist based on mutual trust, the testing of limits and, in the best of cases, the expanding of horizons for all involved. We would like to express our sincere gratitude to Mircea Cantor, for embarking on this journey with us, for engaging so fully with the opportunity presented to him and for producing such a powerful new body of work for so many to see.

The 3 series has been made possible through Arts Council England's Grants for the Arts awards. We are immensely grateful for the Arts Council's support of this innovative project. We would like to thank Marjorie Althorpe-Guyton, formerly Head of Arts at Arts Council England, for her early encouragement of the idea, and especially Elizabeth Gilmore and Sally Abbott at Arts Council South East, who championed our vision. The Romanian Cultural Institute, London, under the guidance of Director Gabriela Massaci and Project Manager Simona Nastac, and The Ratiu Foundation UK, led by Chairman Nicolae Ratiu and Projects Director Ramona Mitrica, have generously supported Mircea Cantor's presentation of *The Need for Uncertainty* in Oxford, Bristol and London, for which we are grateful.

The invitation to Mircea Cantor and to the artists who will follow in the series has resulted from sustained periods of research and discussion between the curatorial teams of our respective institutions: at Modern Art Oxford, led by Suzanne Cotter, Senior Curator; at Arnolfini, by Nav Haq, Exhibitions Curator; and at Camden Arts Centre by Bruce Haines and Anne-Marie Watson, Exhibitions Organisers. Martin Clarke, formerly Curator at Arnolfini, and Sarah Martin, formerly Exhibitions Organiser at Camden were also central to early discussions.

A project of this scale would not be possible without the commitment and skills of many. We would like to express special thanks to Michel Mathelin who worked closely with Mircea Cantor on the production of *The Need for Uncertainty*. In realising the commission, we would also like thank the following people for their assistance, advice and support: Tanya Barson, Olivier Belot, Victoria and Izidor Berbecaru, Martin Caunce, Caroline Collier, Sam Forster, Pop Gheorghe, Hilary Gresty, Paul Hobson, Dvir Intrato, Shifra Shalit Intrato, Andy Keate, Nick Lindsay, Costanza Mazzonis di Pralafera, Mélanie Meffrer-Rondeau, Aurélien Mole, John Norwich, David Preston, Quinton Spratt, Gavin Stenton, Prof. Gheorghe Vanga, and Bârsan Vasile.

In thinking about how we would communicate the series, we have looked to develop an identity that would highlight the collaborative nature of the project, which we have sought to foster on every level. We extend our thanks and appreciation to Simon Josebury, who has worked closely with us on the concept and design of our print material and this publication.

Our final thank you goes to the dedicated teams at Modern Art Oxford, Arnolfini and Camden who, individually and collectively, have and will continue to be vital to the series over its course.

ANDREW NAIRNE, *Director*, SUZANNE COTTER, *Senior Curator*, Modern Art Oxford
TOM TREVOR, *Director*, Arnolfini, Bristol
JENNI LOMAX, *Director*, Camden Arts Centre, London

PAST WORKS

No title
2005
Plexiglass box, newspaper

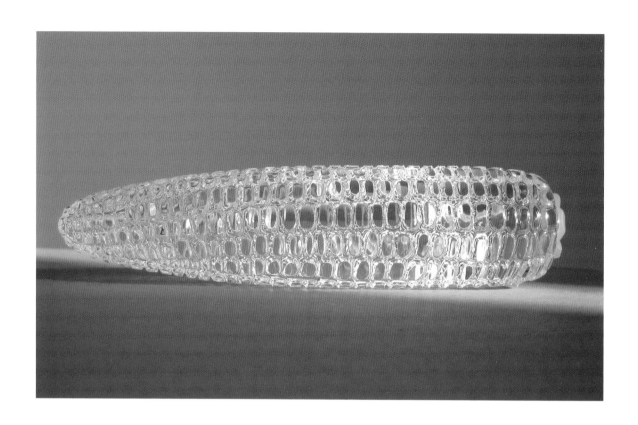

Diamond Corn
2005
Cast crystal, cardboard

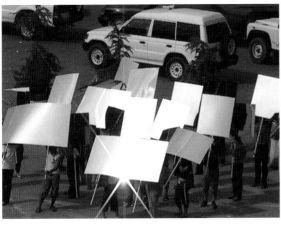

The landscape is changing
2003
Colour film with sound

Deeparture
2005
16mm transferred to BETA digital, colour, silent

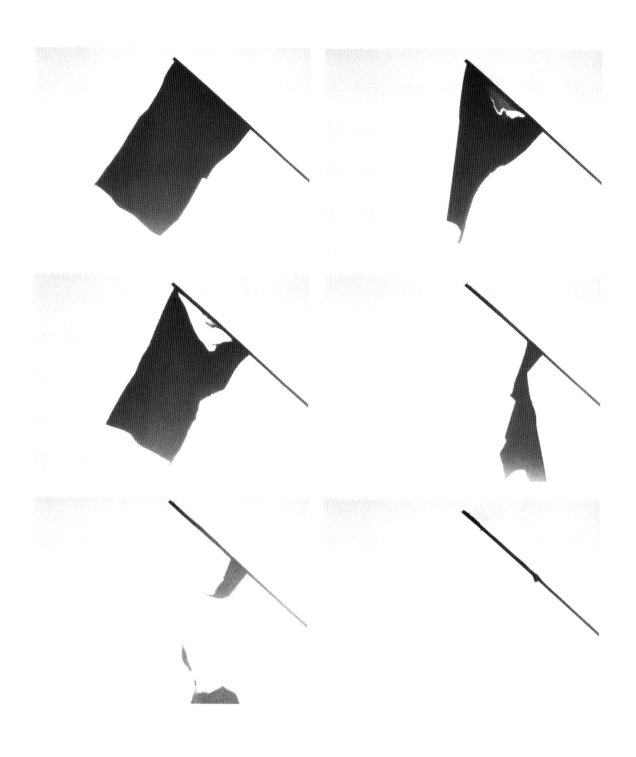

Shadow for a while
2007
16mm b/w film

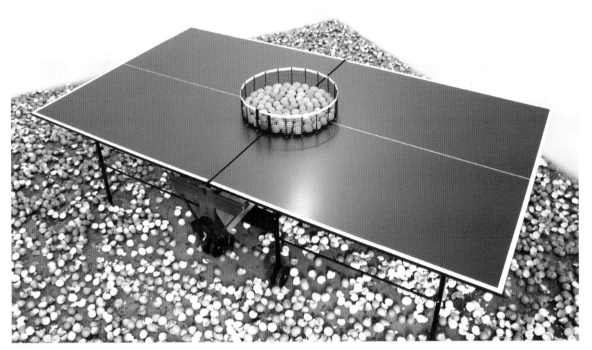

Nido
2007
Ping-pong table, metal elements, eggs

With a free smile
2007
Terracotta

Rosace
2007
Drink cans, plexiglass, aluminium

Stranieri
2007
Bread, knives, salt, hand-made wooden table, paint

IF YOU HOLD YOUR BREATH

My interest in uncertainty is related to the present and the ability to assimilate surprise. We look for transparency and predictability in everything these days. There's a lack of trust about everything. We want to prove, to know, to be certain. There is an inflation of the value of certainty; we need the opposite. This is where artists can play a role.[1]

Uncertainty runs through Mircea Cantor's work like an energy field of charged potential. In Cantor's view, to admit uncertainty is to be open to its possibility as a creative force for thinking and seeing the world. Harbinger of a change in mood, or a shift in time or in place, Cantor's art is one of displacement, in which co-existent planes of perception are repositioned and held in suspense. With Cantor, the single position, be it related to thought, history or society, is dismantled to create a network of equivalences, a question of 'and' rather than 'either/or', of fracturing indeterminacy and wavering certitudes.

As an artist, Cantor feels compelled to respond to contemporary issues, be it the treatment of Romanian immigrants living in different countries, or the visible transformation of cultural traditions in eastern Europe, and in Cantor's native Romania in particular, in the wake of free-market economic models that have prevailed following the collapse of the Soviet Union in 1989. Rather than opt for explicit intervention or a declaration of social or current realities, Cantor relies on the poetic force of his artistic language as a conduit for thinking around ideas and issues that generate multiple reverberations on a visual as well as intellectual level. He has declared that he is "against gratuity and against paraphrase", the simplifying of concepts for the sake of ease and accessibility. Instead, he looks to elicit more complex observations from simple propositions, to create thresholds or, as Mihnea Mircan has observed: "gateways between different versions of the present".

While conscious of Romania's impressive avant-garde artistic lineage, that includes Tristan Tzara, Victor Brauner, Constantin Brancusi, Andrei Cadere, Ion Grigorescu,

Making the 'Airplanes and Angels' carpet in Maramureş, February 2008

and a more recent generation who have emerged since the 1990s – Dan and Lia Perjovschi and Victor Man among others – Cantor is nevertheless at pains to distinguish his position as an artist from his identity:

Artists are a like a sponge. Wherever you put it, it absorbs moisture. I am sensitive to certain realities that can become the source of inspiration for a work. I'm not so interested in making a specific Romanian statement. Through my understanding of what is happening today, and my position in the chain of artistic thought, I can come up with certain ideas that can have an impact.

Characteristic of Cantor's approach to his art is a concern for truthfulness over production value combined with an interest in varied fields of experience that might give form to a particular idea. In previous works and installations, Cantor has used simple, even humble materials and methods to make resonant statements, often relating to the economy of labour and the use of time. He features in a number of his early photographic works, in which he offers his services (*I sell my free time*, 2006), or is sympathetic to, if not complicit with, the inventive economies of marginalised members of society forced to live off the trust and good will of others (*Smen*, 2002).

Statements of a more expansive tenor are expressed with the simplest of gestures.

Thoughts come to him – the pressing of his son's fingertips on a mirror – the arrangement of some shells on a table. With the touch of a pen, an iconic newspaper banner becomes the cipher for multiple histories (*Les Mondes*, 2005). A rural staple is transformed into a cut crystal object of exquisite beauty (*Diamond Corn*, 2005), its humble origins anchored in the simple cardboard plinth on which it is placed, while filming the shadow of a piece of burning cloth (*Shadow for a while*, 2007) sparks a myriad of associations, with history and failed aspirations, with revolutions and their demise.

In more recent works, it is through the mark of the artist, not as a body, but as a symbol of humanity, that simple pronouncements are made: a steam-filled window pane bears the trace of the words 'Unpredictable Future'; 'Ciel Variable', a French translation of a Romanian meteorological term ('Cer Variabil') denoting changeable weather, is written across a ceiling with candle soot. Cantor's fingerprints dipped in printer's ink mark the perimeter of a space to become part rosary, part accusation (*Chaplet*, 2007).

In making what is possibly his most widely known work, *Deeparture*, 2005, Cantor had a deer and a wolf transported to the pristine space of a contemporary art gallery and recorded on film in the closed environment. The resultant documentation of the encounter is compelling in the sense of anticipation it arouses in the viewer. Dualities of predator and prey and of natural instincts bound by a human intervention are undermined by what might be described as an innate complicity against the context that menaces both animals. Within the triangulation of perceptual relationships that emerges, assumptions about co-existence and the imposition of ideologies, as symbolised by the civilising environment of the gallery, are thrown into disarray.

Cantor's directness and simplicity of means brings to mind the use of everyday and elemental materials by Arte Povera artists in the late 1960s, Jannis Kounellis, Michelangelo Pistoletto and Luciano Fabro among them. While these artists emerged onto the Italian and international art scene at a time of a rising centralisation of European consumer culture, Cantor belongs to a generation of artists to have matured amidst the rise of globalisation and free-market economies. Cantor also shares with this earlier moment a predisposition towards live animals in his work, albeit to different uses. Whereas Kounellis used birds and, most famously, horses in his work, they were, according to the artist, intended to operate as compositional elements within an expanded definition of painting (the

brute presence of these imposing animals tethered to the walls of an exhibition space over a period of days has an altogether other immediacy). Telescoping back to the present, Cantor's use of animals, or any other means or material undermines preconceived notions of position and context through the encounter with other levels of cognitive reality.

The Need for Uncertainty grew out of a two-fold preoccupation with the importance of the unpredictable and the idea of freedom and its limitations. As the realisation of an idea, the physical and formal language of the work, which comprises a series of interrelated elements, is one of encryption, overlap and containment, expressed within a visual flow of pattern and repetition: the double helix of the DNA molecule, a peacock and his mate in a series of large golden cages, traditional carpet weaving from north-eastern Romania, and a mysterious, geometric lattice of carved wood with, at its core, the trunk of a tree in the middle of a forest in deepest winter.

In summer 2007, while staying in Cluj Napoca, Cantor visited the region of Maramureş in the north of Romania. Situated on the eastern slopes of the Carpathians and bordered by Hungary and Ukraine, Maramureş is famous for its landscape of rolling hills and picturesque villages, its wooden churches dating from the 19th and early 20th century and the majestic gates carved out of oak and sculpted with protective symbols that herald the entrance to important houses. Maramureş is also known for its elegant woven carpets, made from locally spun and dyed wool and renowned for their harmony of colour and pattern. The talismanic forms and symbols used in both the carvings and the carpets have pre-Christian origins. While many of Romania's historic villages and centres, Bucharest among them, were destroyed under communism, Maramureş was left largely untouched. In recent years, the region has succumbed to the pressures of speculation with many of the wooden houses and gates being sold and dismantled for their wood, which has become a sought-after export (it seems that the particularly dry oak from the traditional houses of Maramureş makes for wonderful parquet floors).

Cantor describes the subsequent development of his own lexicon of forms inspired by Maramureş as a continuation of certain visual traditions in a contemporary way:

I have no nostalgia about tradition. I'm more interested in how to express certain ideas with tools from different fields of knowledge that make sense in the contemporary world.

That the materials and visual texture of pattern and decoration of Maramureş is inseparable from a rich heritage of symbolic function was equally significant to Cantor for whom the relationship between the physical and the metaphysical is paramount. Cantor saw an immediate relationship between the motif of 'the tree of life', carved to resemble the interconnecting strands of thick rope on the face of the vertical supports of Maramureş's wooden gates, and that most contemporary of representations, the double helix of the DNA molecule.

In discussing the collaborative process involved in realising the different elements that make up *The Need for Uncertainty*, Cantor was keen to discern between collaboration as a means and as an end:

When you speak about collaboration today, it's very superficial. I'm curious about other people and what I can learn from them. It's important for me to meet people who produce these forms because it gives a new face to my ideas. In Maramureş, I spent hours, then days, then months speak-ing with the different people I worked with. It wasn't simply a commercial exchange. My relationship with these people, speak-ing with them, learning from them, created an extended energy. These people spent time with me. I'm interested in the material quality of that action of spending time. I believe it's translated in the knowledge they have passed on into the work. It's the same for the carpet, the sculpture, the gate. The relationships that were made during this time went beyond a simple transaction. They marked the beginning of something. After we had completed our work together, Gheorghe Pop, who made the sculpture around the tree and the model for the gate, said to me: "I know we will meet again in the future".

The Need for Uncertainty is also the title of the vast set of cages with peacocks from which the exhibition takes it title. In a visual echo of *Deeparture*, Cantor enacts an extravagant act of displacement that, when experienced in present time and space, is physically and psychologically unsettling. True to what might be described as a Cantoresque conceptual texture, there is an air of enchantment and the fabulous, bordering on the Baroque, in coming across these exotic birds in their compound of golden cages. The physical impact of the cages, heightened by the repetition of vertical bars as they arc upwards, and the jolting awareness of the animals in a space not normally their own, creates a palpable tension. Within the labyrinthine space of the concentric enclosures, the peacock and his mate become, somehow, more present and more demanding of our distance in their muted steps and their silent yet watchful companionship.

Two other forms elaborate further on the idea of worlds within worlds. Suspended in the air in an undulating rhythm is *Airplanes and Angels*, a woven carpet with the figures of airplanes and angels realised in subtle tones of greys, ochres and creams. To make the carpet, Cantor commissioned one of Maramureş's most established weavers, Victoria Berbecaru. Cantor designed the colour scheme and the pattern, based on a mixture of traditional and contemporary motifs. The composition is inspired by traditional carpets of the region and comprises a central ground with distinct borders of decorative bands symbolising water flowing, wolves' teeth, butterflies and the sun and the moon. In the centre of the carpet is a radiating pattern of geometric motifs meant to symbolise rams' horns. Within the remaining field, Cantor introduced the more recent flying figures, which he translated into graphic form by way of Photoshop.

The carpet embodies two distinct forms of investment, that of the time and knowledge of the carpet makers, evident in the weave and texture of the finished object, and the degrees of significance we might ascribe to the aerial forms, be they agents of intercession or destruction. Once again, the scenario pitches us somewhere between allegory and reality. In describing the process of making the carpet and its possible meaning Cantor notes:

With the carpet my interest was not to copy an existing tradition, but rather to update it with my own vision. For this reason I drew in the airplanes and the angels. You will never see airplanes or angels in Romanian rugs. It was more like the dichotomy between two realities, the visible and the invisible. On top of this, you have the association of the Oriental flying carpet. Ideals of flying and traversing the space are deeply rooted in humankind's aspirations. From birds, butterflies and other creatures we always tried to symbolise and copy in a very concrete way their freedom of movement. Today when flying UFOs are no longer taboo, and angels are far more mythical creatures, airplanes seem more meaningful to us. But is it really like this?

The photographic print, *Hiatus*, the third element in Cantor's installation, is an image-space of almost magical disconnection relative to the physical embodiment of time and labour in the carpet and the more-than-reality of the birds in their cages. Once again, a strange duality subtends the very fabric of the work, which exists both as the image and as the carving installed around a tree in a particular place. Cantor worked over a period of several months with a local woodcarver

from Maramureş to make the structure, based on a scaled-up version of traditional wool spindle decorations from the region. The spindle decoration has specific folk origins and associations. Traditionally carved by shepherds during the winter months, the spindles were used by the women of the community who would sit together to spin the wool. The lattice-like construction of the carved decoration produces a rattling sound with the movement of the spindle. Describing his interest in the form, Cantor has declared:

The inspiration was the spindle and its movement. Normally, this form would be in constant vibration as the women spun the wool. I wanted to put a stop to the movement. By putting it in a forest where you would never to see it I also wanted to express the idea of human intelligence amidst the forces of nature, like the black cube that lands in the desert among the apes in 2001: A Space Odyssey.

A fourth element destined to complete the cycle of works is a replica of a Maramureş gate, constructed on a scale of 1:1 and carved by the woodcarver Vasile Bârsan. Cantor envisages covering the monumental form with a layer of gold leaf, which promises to endow it with the immaterial presence we might associate with religious icons and reliquaries. Again, Cantor has defined the representational menu, superimposing a graphic representation of the DNA strand over the symbolic vernacular of the tree of life. Cantor sees the DNA strand as both symbolising the desire for certainty and what he describes as "the continuation of tradition" in another form:

The image of DNA is a symbol of aspiration, a step towards a new world. For this reason, I wanted to put it on the gate. It relates to the pre-Christian symbolism of the tree of life, the solar and celestial symbols. I wanted to update these signs so that people could walk through a new gate; it's a passage towards a new reality.

Both the traditional motifs of protection and the graphic representation of the DNA strand imply structures of logic; both imply transfer of knowledge, between traditions handed from one generation to the next, on the one hand, and on the other, a recognisable code that defines our genetic make-up. Paradoxically, the DNA double helix is more easily graspable as a symbol than as the seemingly fantastic reality that it is – that our make-up is based on the sequencing of protein molecules. Despite the claim of an intellectual revolution that would pave the way for a whole new field of personalised and predictive medicine, the study of DNA has not been shown to change our view of the world and, indeed, of what it is to be human.[3]

Cantor's encounter with the visual language of Maramureş's material culture was part of a sequence of what he describes as "meaningful coincidences":

If I was making a carpet to be woven in Maramureş, it was due to a kind of synchronicity that the woodcarvers for the sculpture in the forest and the gate happened to be in the same region.

The concept of synchronicity is an important one for Cantor. Originally articulated by the psychoanalyst Carl Jung, it describes the relationship between the mind and the phenomenal world of perception as one that operates according to its own logic and is not structured as one of cause and effect.

In merging the local knowledge of craftsmen and women from a particular area of the world with the expanded knowledge of our genetic make-up now shared by humankind, Cantor set in motion a further dynamic of coincidence that is reflected in the elements that make up *The Need for Uncertainty*. Cantor's initial ideas included a giant DNA strand made from solid gold safety pins, a decoration for spindles traditionally used by women to spin wool, and an image of a concentric configuration of boats and their surrounding oceans, creating a concentric pattern of relative horizons. Cantor explains: "It's a question of how to translate ideas that have nothing necessarily to do with the material". Describing one of his early working drawings, a stylised sequence of the DNA strand using lipstick kisses on a sheet of paper, he observed: "The DNA kiss is related to the idea of a vibration."

Cantor's *modus operandi* of equivalence, subject to seemingly endless variation, reflects his sensitivity to the fissile nature of our contemporary present, in which the partial and the relative is privileged over the whole and the fixed. While uncertainty is a mood which prevails in much of the work being produced by a current generation of artists, Cantor's sights are not set on retriev- ing past cultural moments – Modernism in particular – as a way of reflecting on an as yet undefined future. Nor is his work infused with the wistful melancholia of many of his peers.[4] It seems more relevant to reflect on the multivalent fields of meaning and association embedded in Cantor's work in terms of knowledge production and belief, and the mechanisms of our technological present. Writing recently on the change in production models for artists, art historian Caroline A. Jones coined the term 'hive mind' to describe these servers and users for whom "knowledge production is construed as inevitably hybrid, mediated, deferred and diffuse".[5] Certainly, the

openness and mutability of interpretation which are to the fore in Cantor's work chimes with our current moment, increasingly subject to the bespoke principles of *Wikipedia*, *You Tube* and the rest.

However, to understand Cantor's art purely in terms of process, production and use, or as a simple transliteration from one realm to another, is to deny the poetic and potentially political charge we might infer from the physical stuff of life, which is at the core of his artistic project. Cantor gives cause for anticipation, to hold your breath, just for a moment and to rethink what it is you thought was certain. His art is to simultaneously capture the world as we know it and to rephrase it within a different order that, while far from certain, is undeniably anew.

1   Mircea Cantor, March 2008. This and subsequent quotes by Cantor are from conversations with the artist in Paris and Oxford between November 2007 and March 2008.

2   Mihnea Mircan, 'The Noise of Contention. On Mircea Cantor's Recent Work', *Mircea Cantor*, Le Collège/Frac Champagne-Ardenne, Yvon Lambert, 2007, p.135.

3   See H. Allen Orr's exposition of the field of genomics in, 'The Genetic Adventurer', *New York Review of Books*, March 20, 2008.

4   The 2008 Berlin Biennial, which opened at the time of writing this text, is a sign of the times in terms of a current generation of artists who are looking to artists and artistic moments in the past, with a sense of uncertainty and not without a certain degree of melancholy. See Elena Filipovic and Adam Szymczyk, *When Things Cast No Shadow, 5th Berlin Biennial for Contemporary Art*, JRP Ringier, 2008.

5   Caroline A. Jones, 'The Server/User Mode', *Artforum*, October 2007.

SUZANNE COTTER

Idea for Oxford, November 2007

Housing block in Sighet

Proposal for a sculpture: golden safety pins in the shape of the DNA spiral

Drawing for gate with the tree of life as DNA

Above and below:
Tree of life as DNA
chain carved as a
traditional wooden
gate from Maramureş
(maquette)

Wooden gate in Vadu Izei, Romania, 2007

Wooden gate carved by Vasile Bârsan, Bârsana, Romania, 2007
Gate pillar from Văleni, Maramureş

Bangkok, January 2008

Candle smoke drawing   DNA kiss, studio, Paris

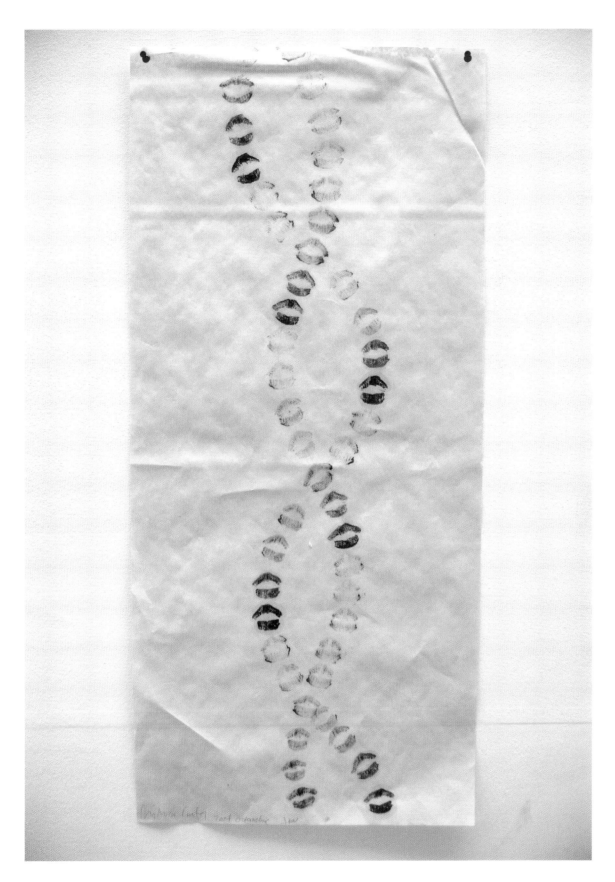

Strap for a traditional wool bag in Maramureş

Tree on Koh Rok island, Thailand

Wool spindles from the Ethnographic Museum in Sighet

Carpet made by Victoria Berbecaru in 1988, Botiza, Maramureş

Carpet from Ieud, Maramureş, made in the 1980s (detail)

THE NEED FOR UNCERTAINTY

This page and overleaf:
The Need for Uncertainty,
Modern Art Oxford
2008
Steel cages, gold paint, peacocks

The Need for Uncertainty
2008
Steel cages, gold paint, peacocks

Airplanes and *Angels*
2008
Hand-woven wool carpet

Hiatus
2008
Lamda print

Installation at Modern Art Oxford

The Need for Uncertainty
2008
(details)

Airplanes and *Angels*, 2008
Previous page: *Hiatus*, 2008

MIRCEA CANTOR

Mircea Cantor was born in 1977 in Romania. He lives between Paris and Cluj and is co-editor of VERSION, an artist-run magazine (www.versionmagazine.com). He was awarded the Prix Paul Ricard S.A., Paris in 2004.

EXHIBITION HISTORY (*catalogue)

Solo Exhibitions

2009
The Need for Uncertainty, Camden Arts Centre, London

2008
The Need for Uncertainty, Modern Art Oxford; Arnolfini, Bristol

2007
Magazzino d'Arte Moderna, Rome
Deeparture, screening, Black Box, Hirshhorn Museum, Washington
A free smile, Galerie Yvon Lambert, New York
Ciel Variable, FRAC Champagne Ardennes, Reims *
Deeparture, screening, Museo Tamayo Arte Contemporaneo, Mexico City
The landscape is changing, screening, Milton Keynes Gallery, Milton Keynes

2006
Jucării pentru copii (Toys for children), with Ion Grigorescu, Protokoll Studio, Cluj Napoca *
The Title Is the Last Thing, Philadelphia Museum of Art *
Born to be Burnt, GAMeC, Galleria d'Arte Moderna e Contemporanea di Bergamo
The landscape is changing, screening, Tel Aviv Museum of Art

2005
Dvir Gallery, Tel Aviv
Prix Ricard S.A., Musée National d'Art Moderne, Centre Georges Pompidou, Paris
Deeparture, Galerie Yvon Lambert, New York
Si tu marche plus vite, il pleut moins fort, Centro de

Arte Moderna, Calouste Gulbenkian Foundation, Lisbon *

2004
Preview, Magazzino d'Arte Moderna, Rome

2003
Corporate identity, FRAC des Pays de la Loire, Carquefou
(...), Galerie Yvon Lambert, Paris
In Front of My Eyes, Trans> area, New York

2002
The Right Man at the Right Place, Galerie Yvon Lambert, Paris
Nulle part ailleurs, Le Studio, Yvon Lambert, Paris
Ping Pang Pong, Entre-deux Association, Nantes *

1999
Headlines, GAD Photogallery, Bucharest

Group Exhibitions

2008
28th Bienal de São Paulo, São Paulo *
Eurasia, Museo di arte moderna e contemporanea di Trento e Rovereto, Rovereto
God and Goods - Spirituality and mass confusion, Villa Manin Centro d'Arte Contemporanea, Codroipo *
Shifting Identities - (Swiss) Art Now, Kunsthaus Zurich *
Locked In, Casino Luxembourg, Luxembourg *
Artes Mundi 3, National Museum Cardiff *
Mimetisme, Extra City, Centrum voor hedendaagse kunst, Antwerp

2007
Taking Time, Museo de Arte Contemporánea de Vigo, Vigo *
Stop. Look. Listen: An Exhibition of Video Works, Johnson Museum of Art, Cornell University, Ithaca
Brave New Worlds, Walker Art Center, Minneapolis *
An Atlas of Events, Calouste Gulbenkian Foundation, Lisbon *
Numerica, Palazzo delle Papesse - Centro Arte

Contemporanea, Siena *
Noise, Poeziezomer 07, Watou *
Critical Foreground, New Langton Arts, San Francisco
Power Play, Artpace, San Antonio
Logiques du rêve éveillé, Instants Chavirés, Montreuil
Airs de Paris, Musée National d'Art Moderne, Centre
Georges Pompidou, Paris *
Hay algo de revolucionario en todo esto, Sala
Parpalló, Valencia
Fairytale, Tirana Institute of Contemporary Art, Tirana
I want to believe, Galerie Eva Presenhuber, Zurich
Confined Innocence, Art Gallery of Windsor, Ontario *
Paranoia, Freud Museum, London *

2006
Bienal Internacional de Arte Contemporáneo de
Sevilla, Seville *
Contos Dixitais, CGAC, Santiago de Compostela
October Art Salon, Belgrade *
I Bienal de Arquitectura, Arte y Paisaje de Canarias,
Canary Islands *
Cluj Connection, Haunch of Venison, Zurich *
Busan Biennial, Busan *
Dada east? The Romanians of Cabaret Voltaire,
Cabaret Voltaire, Zurich
Voices of Silence, Herzliya Museum of Art, Herzliya
Printemps de septembre, Toulouse *
Human Game – Winner and losers, Stazione Leopolda,
Florence *
Paranoia, Leeds City Art Gallery, Leeds *
Whitstable Biennale, Whitstable, Kent
Periferic 7: Focusing Iaşi / Why Children?, Iaşi,
Romania *
Marcher, Maison des Arts Georges Pompidou, Cajarc
LESS Strategie alternative dell'abitare, PAC
Padiglione d'Arte Contemporanea, Milan *
Message Personnel, Galerie Yvon Lambert, Paris *
4th Berlin Biennial for Contemporary Art, Berlin *
Notre Histoire…, Palais de Tokyo, Paris *

2005
Global Tour, Art Travel and Beyond, W139,
Amsterdam *
May you live in interesting times, Cardiff Festival of
Creative Technology, Cardiff
War is over, 1945 – 2005 The Freedom of Art from

Picasso to Warhol and Cattelan, GAMeC - Galleria
d'Arte Moderna e Contemporanea, Bergamo *
Modern Times, Museo d'Arte Provincia di Nuoro,
Nuoro
Nach Rokytník - The EVN Collection, Museum
Moderner Kunst Stiftung Ludwig, Vienna
Generations of art -10 years at F.A.R., Fondazione
Antonio Ratti, Como *
On Difference, Würtembergischer Kunstverein, Stuttgart
Cosmopolis, State Museum for Contemporary Art,
Thessaloniki *
TEXT ground, Display, Space for contemporary art,
Prague *
e-flux video rental, Project Room, KW Institute of
Contemporary Art, Berlin
Revolution is on hold, Isola Art Center, Milan
Theorema, une collection privée en Italie, Musée d'art
contemporain, Collection Lambert, Avignon *
The need to document, Kunsthaus Baselland, Basel *
Works from the collection, Magasin 3 Konsthall,
Stockholm
Universal Experience: Art, Life, and the Tourist's Eye,
Museum of Contemporary Art, Chicago *
Irreducible: contemporary short form video, 1995–
2005, CCA Wattis, San Francisco

2004
The works I told you about, Galerie Yvon Lambert,
Paris
Stock Zero (OPERA), MNAC, National Museum of
Contemporary Art, Bucharest *
Prosismic, Espace Paul Ricard, Paris *
I'll be your Mirror, A special project for Frieze Art Fair
2004, City Inn Westminster Hotel, London
Publishing Without Limits: New Directions for Art
Magazines, Art Forum Berlin Talks (with VERSION)
Cetinje Biennale, Cetinje *
Nine Points of the Law, Neue Gesellschaft für
Bildende Kunst, Berlin *
Mediterraneo, MACRO, Rome
Plug in, Futura, Prague *
Quicksand, De Appel, Amsterdam *
Imagine Limerick, Limerick City Gallery of Art, Limerick
The Happy Worker, Center for Curatorial Studies
Museum, Bard College, Annandale-on-Hudson, New
York

New Video, New Europe: A Survey of Eastern European Video, Renaissance Society, Chicago/ Tate Modern, London

2003
Tirana Biennale 2, National Gallery of Arts, Tirana *
Phalanstère, Centre d'art contemporain, Brétigny
In the Gorges of the Balkans, Kunsthalle Fridericianum, Kassel *
Poesis. The Everyday Differently, Kunsthalle/ Mucsarnok, Budapest *
Displaced, UCLA Hammer Museums, Los Angeles *
50th La Biennale Di Venezia, « *Clandestine* », Venice *
Unoccupied territories, K&S gallery, Berlin *
International Film Festival, Rotterdam *

2002
Les enfants du paradis, Galerie Yvon Lambert, Paris
ForwArt 2002, Brussels
A9 Forum Transeuropa, Museums Quartier, Vienna *
Urban Tension, museum in progress, Brussels; Vienna; Frankfurt; Rome
Boundless Borders, billboards project, Belgrade; Sarajevo; Bucharest; Thessaloniki; Kassel *
Festival Rendez-Vous Roumain, Espace En Cours, Paris * (with VERSION)

2001
Documents.11 young photographers, New Gallery, Bucharest *
Traversées, ARC Musée d'Art Moderne de la Ville de Paris, Paris *
Heimsuchung, FRAC des Pays de la Loire, Carquefou (Context-network), Romanian Pavillion, *49th Biennale Di Venezia*, Venice *
Art Judgment Show, Moderna Galerija, Ljubliana
Jean Pierre Magazine, CNEAI Centre National de l'Estampe et de l'Art Imprimé, Chatou *
Transferatu, Ifa Gallery, Bonn *

2000
Transitioland, Museul National de Arta, Bucharest *
Transferatu, Ifa Gallery, Berlin *
Say What?, Eforie Gallery, Bucharest *
Argos Project 2000, Vevey
Actif-Reactif, C.R.D.C., Nantes *

International Boutique, >Public, Paris
MK2 project café, Paris
Periferic 4, Turkish bath, Iaşi *
One Night Stand, Klemens Gasser & Tanja Grunert Gallery, New York
Voyages d'affaires, with Gabriela Vanga, ERBAN, Nantes *

ARTICLES AND REVIEWS

2008
Alina Purcaru, 'Mircea Cantor şi covoarele', *Cotidianul*, 25 February
Marcello Smarelli, 'Recensioni: Magazzino d'Arte Moderna', *Flash Art Italia*, no.268
Patricia Briggs, 'Previews: Brave New Worlds', *Artforum*, January

2007
Blake Gopnik, 'The Idea: Predator, Prey, Provocative', *Washington Post*, 28 October
Pier Paolo Pancotto, 'Mircea Cantor esce dal "Nido"', *L'Unita*, 29 December
Morgan Falconer, 'A Free Smile', *ArtReview*, November
Cristina Hermeziu, 'O amintire cu Mircea Cantor', *Evenimentul zilei*, 12 August
Sean James Rose, 'Mircea Cantor, poète politique', *Libération*, 12 June
Emanuelle Lequeux, 'Un Autre Monde est Possible - Portrait', *Beaux Arts magazine*, no.275
Marie-Pierre Duquoc, 'All around the worlds', *Revue 303*, no.96
Nick Hackworth, 'Preachiness overpowers poetry', *Evening Standard*, 11 January

2006
Alessando Rabottini, 'A future world', *Flash Art*, no.251
Steven Henry Madoff, 'At Berlin Biennial, Art Fits Everywhere', *The New York Times*, 11 April
Von Harald Fricke, 'Von Wolfen und Rehen', *Die Tageszeitung*, 25 March
Jennifer Allen, 'The 4th Berlin Biennial', *Artforum*, May

Samuel Schellenberg, 'Bienale a la vie, a la mort', *Le Courier*, 29 April
Steffen Dengler, 'Der Wolf lauert uberall', *Abendzeitung München*, 25 March

2005
Christy Lange, 'A story I want to believe', *Parkett*, no.74
Christy Lange, 'Artist meets con artist; Travel and tourism; Matches lit at both ends', *Frieze*, no.95
Travis Jeppesen, 'Read this text', *Umelec Magazine*, no.3
Ami Barak, 'Reviews - Mircea Cantor, Gabriela Vanga', *Artpress*, no.315
Roxana Azimi, 'Marché de l'art. Regard sur la nouvelle Europe', *Le Monde*, 11 September
Ana Maria Onisei, 'Un nou « Version » al artei contemporane', *Suplimentul de Cultură*, Iaşi, no.28
'Dialog între Mircea Cantor şi Cosmin Costinaş', *Dilema Veche*, no.65, 15 April

2004
'Boris Groys talks to Jan Fuchtjohann and Mircea Cantor', *Janus*, no.17
Miriam Bers, 'Her und Hin', *Tema Celeste*, November-December
Florena Dobrescu, 'Mircea Cantor a câştigat Premiul tînărului artist francez', *Adevărul*, 25 October
Francesca Shaw/Lavinia Garulli, 'Was will Europa', *Flash Art International*, no.237
Amiel Grumberg, 'Le guide de Rout'art', *Beaux Arts magazine*, no.242
Simona Vladikova, 'Pictures at an exhibition', *Umelec Magazine*, February
Chiara Leoni, 'Prague gets plugged…', *Flash Art International*, no.236
Amiel Grumberg, 'The landscape is changing', *Quicksand*, De Appel, Amsterdam
Yasmil Raymond Ventura, 'The Happy Worker', unpublished thesis, Bard College, Annandale-on-Hudson

2003
Attila Tordai-S, 'Aperto Romania', *Flash Art International*, no.233
Vanina Pinter, 'L'œuvre à processus', *Etapes*,

November, no.102
Michele Robecchi, 'Tirana Biennial 2', *IDEA arts+society*, no.15+16
Elsa Demo, 'Tirana në pasqyrat e rumunit Cantor', *Shekulli*, no.208
Dan Perjovschi, 'Mircea Cantor Super Star', *IDEA arts+society*, no.14
Thomas Boutoux, 'Ouverture', *Flash Art International*, no.229
Ami Barak, 'Mircea Cantor and the match theory', *Balkon*, no.13
'Dossier: 10 vidéastes en vue', *Beaux Arts magazine*, no.224

2002
Anne Pontégnie, 'On the road again', *ForwArt* catalogue, Brussels
'Ping Pang Pong', flip book, *Entre-deux Association* (ed.), Nantes
Léa Gauthier, 'Ecrans de fantasme', *Mouvement*, no.16, April-June
'Traversări, Mircea Cantor; Interview with Hans Ulrich Obrist', *Balkon*, no.10
Olivier Michelon, 'Je ne suis plus un étudiant. Les post-diplômes en France', *Le Journal des Arts*, no.142
Hans Ulrich Obrist, 'First Take', *Artforum*, January

2001
Magda Cârneci, 'Travesând Traversées', *Artelier*, no.7
Elena Deldrago, 'Piccoli miracoli della provincia francese', *Il Manifesto*, 11 December
Jean Max Collard, 'Nouvelles frontières', *Inrockuptibles*, no.312
Stefanie Stadel, 'Rumänien: der Zukunft zugewandt', *Kunstzeitung*, no.57, May
Catherine Millet, 'Transitioland', *Artpress*, no.268

MIRCEA CANTOR
THE NEED FOR UNCERTAINTY

MODERN ART OXFORD
2 April - 1 June 2008
Curated by
Suzanne Cotter, Senior Curator
Assisted by
Emily Smith, Associate Assistant Curator
Tom Procter-Legg, Gallery Manager

ARNOLFINI, BRISTOL
13 September - 16 November 2008
Curated by
Nav Haq, Exhibitions Curator

CAMDEN ARTS CENTRE, LONDON
13 February - 12 April 2009
Curated by
Bruce Haines, Exhibitions Organiser, and Anne-Marie
Watson, Exhibitions Organiser
Assisted by
Richard Gough, Gallery Manager

Published by Modern Art Oxford, Arnolfini, Bristol,
Camden Arts Centre, London
Edited by Suzanne Cotter and Emily Smith

Publication design: Secondary Modern, London
Photography for *The Need for Uncertainty* by
Andy Keate

Printed by Lecturis, Eindhoven, in an edition of 1600
Stock: Zanders Ikono Silk
Font: Adobe Futura Bold/Light

Distributed in the UK by
Cornerhouse
70 Oxford Street
Manchester M1 5NH
England
T. +44 (0) 161 200 1503
F. +44 (0) 161 200 1504
E: publications@cornerhouse.org
www.cornerhouse.org/publications

Photographic credits
pp.17, 20, 21 © Aurélien Mole
pp.44 © Lorand Bartha
All other images © Mircea Cantor

ISBN 978-1-901352-36-8

ARTIST'S ACKNOWLEDGEMENTS:
I would like to thank Suzanne Cotter for her patience,
dialogue and time on the preparation of this
commission and its subsequent exhibition. I would
like to thank deeply all those who helped generously
in the realisation of the pieces for *The Need for
Uncertainty*, among them: Prof. Gheorghe Vanga,
Michel Mathelin, Victoria and Izidor Berbecaru, Pop
Gheorghe, Aurélien Mole, Bârsan Vasile, and Stella
Smulevitz. I would also like to thank Tom Procter-Legg,
Emily Smith, Allia Ali, Sara Dewsbery and Kirsty Kelso
for their support on the production of the exhibition,
and Simon Josebury for his receptivity and creative
work in the making of this catalogue.

MIRCEA CANTOR
THE NEED FOR UNCERTAINTY

MODERN ART OXFORD
30 Pembroke Street, Oxford OX1 1BP
Tel: + 44 (0) 1865 722 733
Fax: + 44 (0) 1865 722 573
www.modernartoxford.org.uk

ARNOLFINI
16 Narrow Quay, Bristol BS1 4QA
Tel: 44 (0) 117 917 2300
Fax: 44 (0) 117 917 2303
www.arnolfini.org.uk

CAMDEN ARTS CENTRE
Arkwright Road, London NW3 6DG
Tel +44 (0) 20 7472 5500
Fax +44 (0) 20 7472 5501
www.camdenartscentre.org

MODERN ART OXFORD
ARNOLFINI
Camden arts centre

III 3 artists 3 spaces 3 years
is funded by the National Lottery through Arts Council
England. Mircea Cantor The Need for Uncertainty is
supported by the Romanian Cultural Institute in London
and the Ratiu Foundation UK.